HAMILTON COLLEGE

D0349122

What's for lunch?

HAMILTON COLLEGE

Sweetcorn

© 1997 Franklin Watts
96 Leonard Street
London
EC2A 4RH

Franklin Watts Australia
14 Mars Road
Lane Cove
NSW 2066

ISBN 0 7496 2803 0

Dewey Decimal Classification Number 641.3

A CIP catalogue record for this book is available from
the British Library

Editor: Samantha Armstrong
Series designer: Kirstie Billingham
Designer: Dalia Hartman
Consultant: Anne Stone
Reading Consultant: Prue Goodwin, Reading and Language
Information Centre, Reading

Printed in Hong Kong

What's for lunch?

Sweetcorn

Pam Robson

W
FRANKLIN WATTS
NEW YORK • LONDON • SYDNEY

Today we are having sweetcorn for lunch.

Sweetcorn is a vegetable.

Sometimes we eat sweetcorn
as corn-on-the-cob.

Sweetcorn contains sugar and **starch**.

Eating sweetcorn will give you **energy**.

Sweetcorn comes from a plant called maize.

Maize can be very colourful.

Some maize is green, brown, red, or purple.

Maize is also used to make popcorn,

cornflakes and animal food.

Maize grows in many different countries.
Some kinds of maize grow best
in hot places like Brazil.

Other kinds grow best in cooler places,
like Nebraska in America.
Most of the maize we eat comes from America.
In America, maize is called corn.

Like all plants,
maize must have water
and sunshine to grow.
In hot countries,
maize seeds are planted
when there is plenty of rain.
In cooler countries,
the seeds are planted
in the Spring.
A large machine
sows the seeds in the soil.

Farmers put **fertilizer**
on the soil to help the
maize grow strong.
Insects sometimes
eat the growing plants.
Aeroplanes spray
the **crop** with
insecticide to
kill the insects.

Maize has both male and female flowers.
The wind blows **pollen** from the
male flowers to the female flowers.
The female flowers have threads
called **silks** to collect the pollen.
The pollen makes seeds grow
inside the female flowers.
The female flowers are covered with
special leaves called **husks** to protect them.

The seeds are called **kernels**.
The kernels grow on a **cob**.
Some types of maize have
soft, sweet kernels.
When the kernels are yellow,
a machine snaps the cobs
off the plant.
When we eat maize
at this stage it is called
"corn-on-the-cob".

Sometimes we take the kernels off the cob.
We call the kernels "sweetcorn".

Sweetcorn usually tastes best when it is fresh.
So it is quickly packed into tins, or else frozen.

Sometimes maize is treated
in a different way.
A machine called a
harvester picks the cobs
from the plants.
Then the husks
are removed and
the kernels are taken out.
We call this **threshing**.

The maize goes to mills where machines clean it, dry it and grind it.
The ground maize is made into animal food, glue, or cornflour.
It can be finely ground into **corn meal** to use in cooking.
It is also used to make cornflakes.

glue

Sweetcorn and maize products often travel many miles before being eaten.
Tins of sweetcorn and boxes of cornflour are packed on trains and ships and planes.
When they arrive, they are taken to the shops.
There they are put on shelves for us to buy.

Many different products
come from maize.
Corn oil is used for cooking.
Popcorn comes from kernels
that have been dried
and are heated up until they pop.
Corn chips are crunchy.

Maize is eaten all around the world.
In Mexico, corn meal is used to make
crispy pancakes called taco shells.
Delicious fillings are put inside them.

28

In America corn muffins
are often eaten for breakfast.
Maize is a very useful plant.

Glossary

cob　　　　the hard centre of corn on which the seeds, or kernels, of sweetcorn grow

cornflour　a smooth white flour made from ground maize

corn meal　a yellow flour made from crushed grains of maize

crop　　　　what farmers grow in their fields

energy　　the strength to work and play

fertilizer　something that helps plants to grow

harvester　a large machine that cuts down the maize plant and removes the cobs from the plant

husk	the outside covering of a fruit or seed
insecticide	something that kills insects
kernel	a seed of corn inside the husk
pollen	powder made by male flowers which fertilizes the female flowers
silk	a tuft growing on the female flower of the maize plant
starch	a white substance found in certain foods such as potatoes, rice and sweetcorn
threshing	separating the grains of corn from the husk
vegetable	a plant grown for the parts that can be eaten

HAMILTON
COLLEGE

Index

cobs 17, 18, 21
corn 9
corn-on-the-cob 5, 17

farmers 13
fertilizer 13
flowers 14

husks 14, 21

insects 13

kernels 17, 18, 21, 26

maize 6, 8, 9, 10, 17, 21, 22, 25, 26, 28, 29

sweetcorn 5, 6, 18, 19, 25

Picture credits: Eye Ubiquitous 12 (Adrian Carroll); By kind permission of Green Giant ® 18, 19; Holt Studios International 6 (Inga Spence), 10-11 (Willem Harinck), 13 (Len McLeod), 14 (Nigel Cattlin), 15 (Nigel Cattlin), 16-7 (Nigel Cattlin), 20-1 (Willem Harinck), 24 (Inga Spence); Images 7, 8-9; Nick Bailey Photography cover, 3, 5. All other photographs Tim Ridley, Wells Street Studio, London. **With thanks to Lois Browne and Ushil Patel.**